EDGE BOOKS™

Imagine It, Build It

Cool

CARDBOARD

PROJECTS

You Can
Create

by Marne Ventura

CAPSTONE PRESS
a capstone imprint

Edge Books are published by Capstone Press,
1710 Roe Crest Drive, North Mankato, Minnesota 56003
www.capstonepub.com

Library of Congress Cataloging-in-Publication Data
Ventura, Marne, author.
Cool cardboard projects you can create / by Marne Ventura.
pages cm.—(Edge books. Imagine it, build it)
Summary: "Simple step-by-step instructions teach readers how to make original
projects from cardboard"—Provided by publisher.
Audience: Ages 8–12.
Audience: Grades 4 to 6.
Includes bibliographical references.
ISBN 978-1-4914-4291-3 (library binding)
ISBN 978-1-4914-4327-9 (eBook PDF)
1. Paper work—Juvenile literature. 2. Paperboard—Juvenile literature.
3. Handicraft—Juvenile literature. I. Title.
TT870.V457 2016
745.54—dc23   2015001411

Editorial Credits
Aaron Sautter, editor; Ted Williams, designer; Sarah Schuette, studio stylist;
Marcy Morin, studio scheduler; Laura Manthe, production specialist

Photo Credits
All photographs by Capstone Studio: Karon Dubke

Design Elements
Shutterstock: Alhovik, M.E. Mulder, slava17, Sharon Day, Tischenko Irina

Printed in the United States of America in North Mankato, Minnesota.
062015   008823CGF15

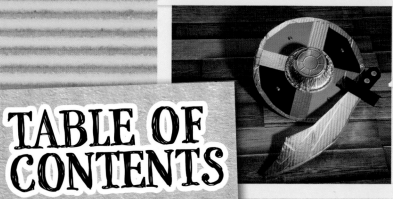

TABLE OF CONTENTS

Construct Awesome Cardboard Projects!

What do cereal boxes, shoe boxes, and paper towel tubes all have in common? They're all made from cardboard! Before cardboard was invented, people often used heavy wooden crates for storage and shipping. But when cardboard boxes were created in the 1870s, it was a major step forward for storing and shipping goods. The boxes were strong, lightweight, and cheap.

Today cardboard isn't just used to make boxes. If you look around your home you'll probably find many things made of cardboard. And the great thing about it is you don't have to throw cardboard into the recycling bin. You can use it to make fun projects instead!

Look around for some boxes, tubes, and other cardboard objects. When you're ready, just follow the step-by-step instructions. Soon you'll be building robots, armor, weapons, and other awesome cardboard projects to impress your friends!

Tools Needed

You'll need some common tools to make many of your projects. Gather the following tools and store them in a box so they're easy to find when you need them. Remember to always ask an adult for help when using sharp knives, scissors, or hot glue guns.

scissors

utility knife

hot glue gun

paintbrush

hole punch

cutting board

ruler

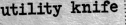

yardstick

Tips and Tricks

» Get a good cutting mat. Craft stores sell mats with grid lines that help make measuring easy. A wood or plastic cutting board and a ruler will also work well.

» Before starting a project, read through all of the steps and be sure to gather all the necessary materials.

» For large projects ask people at your local appliance store if they have any big boxes you can use.

Groovy Guitar

Are you ready for some rock 'n' roll? **Using cardboard, some rubber bands, and a plastic lid, you can make an awesome guitar with a fun, boingy sound. Call a few friends and get ready to rock out!**

MATERIALS

- 5 sheets of corrugated cardboard, 10 by 30 inches (25 by 76 centimeters)
- 3-inch (7.6-cm) wide plastic lid from potato chip container
- 1/8-inch (0.3-cm) wide dowel, 16 inches (41 cm) long
- 4 rubber bands, 7 inches (18 cm) long
- large paper clips
- acrylic paint
- 3 water bottle caps
- drill and 1/8-inch (0.3-cm) drill bit

Step 1: Measure and mark guitar shapes on a sheet of cardboard. The body should measure 10 by 15 inches (25 by 38 cm). The guitar neck should measure 2 by 11 inches (5 by 28 cm). Mark a 3- by 4-inch (7.6- by 10-cm) rectangle on the end of the neck for the guitar head. Cut out the guitar shapes. Use them as patterns to cut out four more body and neck shapes.

Step 2: Use the lid as a pattern to draw a circle in the center of four guitar body shapes. Cut out the circles.

Step 3: Hot glue the cardboard pieces with holes together. Be sure the sound holes line up with one another. Glue the last body piece that has no hole to the back of the guitar.

Step 4: Paint the front and back of the guitar. Let it dry completely. Add frets to the neck piece with a marker.

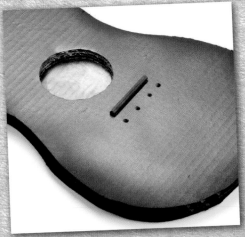

Step 5: Measure 1 inch (2.5 cm) from the bottom of the sound hole. Mark a 2.5-inch (6.4-cm) long line at this spot. Measure and mark a 1.5-inch (3.8-cm) long line at the top of the guitar neck. Make a small slit along each line. Place a 2.5-inch (6.4-cm) and a 1.5-inch (3.8-cm) long piece of dowel in the slits and glue them in place.

Step 6: Measure and mark four evenly spaced holes below the sound hole about 0.5 inch (1.3 cm) below the dowel. Measure and mark four more holes about 0.5 inch (1.3 cm) above the dowel in the neck piece. Ask an adult to help you drill 1/8-inch (0.3-cm) wide holes through the guitar at the marks.

Step 7: Snip the rubber bands so they are straight pieces instead of loops. Thread one rubber band through each bottom hole at the back of the guitar. Tie the end of each rubber band to one large paper clip. Turn over the guitar and pull the rubber bands snugly. Thread the other ends of the rubber bands through the top set of holes. Tie the ends to a second paper clip. The paper clips should be snug against the back of the guitar to help hold the rubber bands firmly in place.

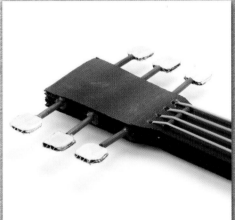

Step 8: Cut six 1.5-inch (3.8-cm) long pieces of dowel. Hot glue three of them on each side of the guitar head. Glue key-shaped cardboard cutouts to the ends of the dowels.

Step 9: Glue the three water bottle caps to the lower side of the guitar body for volume and tone control buttons. Now you're ready to rock out!

Tip: Make your guitar look even cooler by painting on lightning bolts or flames.

Incredible Life-Size Robot

Need a place to post your baseball schedule or send a message to your little brother? Just use this awesome cardboard android assistant! Have fun using dry erase markers to write messages to your family on the whiteboard body.

MATERIALS

- 1 large square cardboard box
- 1 medium square cardboard box
- 2 medium rectangular cardboard boxes
- masking tape
- silver duct tape
- 2 pieces of dryer vent hose, 20 inches (51 cm) long
- silver spray paint
- whiteboard paint
- black markers
- metal nuts, washers, bottle caps, and other objects

Step 1: Tape the cardboard boxes shut with masking tape. Place the rectangular boxes to form the robot's feet and legs. Use the large square box for the robot's chest. Use the medium square box for its head. Hot glue the boxes together. Paint the entire robot with silver spray paint and allow to dry.

Step 2: Cut holes in the sides of the chest box to fit the dryer vent hoses. Place the hoses in the holes and hot glue them in place. Tape around the joints with silver duct tape. Fold a piece of tape around the other ends of the hoses to smooth the edges.

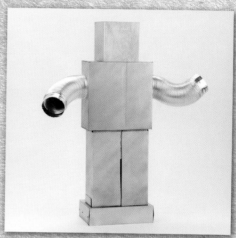

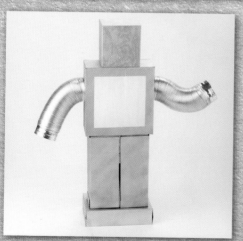

Tip: You can also paint an old pair of goggles to make cool robot eyes.

Step 3: Outline a large square on the robot's chest with masking tape. Paint this square with whiteboard paint and allow to dry. When the paint is dry, remove the tape.

Step 4: Use black markers to outline the robot's feet, legs, and message box. Attach nuts, washers, bottle caps, and other objects with hot glue to create the robot's face and controls.

11

Viking Shield and Sword

Fierce Viking warriors charged into battle with sturdy shields and swords. With just a few simple supplies, you can make your own cardboard sword and shield. Make several of these with your friends and stage your own epic adventure!

MATERIALS

- 1 large pizza pan
- 3 large flat sheets of cardboard
- black and gold paint
- 1 small aluminum or paper bowl
- silver and black duct tape
- clean milk jug with handle
- 4 buttons or bottle caps
- 1-inch (2.5-cm) wide dowel, 18 inches (46 cm) long
- fake jewels

Step 1: Trace around the pizza pan onto the large sheet of cardboard. Cut out the circle. Draw a large X on the cardboard circle to divide it into four sections. Paint the sections black and gold.

Step 2: Place strips of silver duct tape along the lines of the X. Fold duct tape around the edge of the shield.

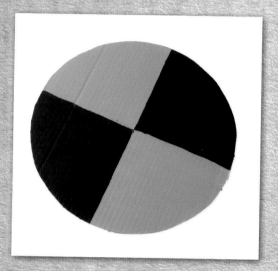

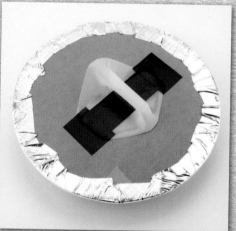

Step 3: Hot glue the small aluminum bowl upside down onto the center of the shield. Or cover a paper bowl with silver duct tape and glue it to the shield.

Step 4: Cut the handle off the milk jug. Hot glue it to the center of the back of the shield. Use duct tape to help make the handle stronger.

13

Step 5: Draw an 18-inch (46-cm) long sword shape on two sheets of cardboard. Include a 4-inch (10-cm) wide cross guard and a rounded pommel at the bottom. Cut out the sword pieces.

Step 6: Attach the dowel to the inside of one cardboard sword shape with duct tape. Then hot glue the two sword shapes together with the dowel inside.

Step 7: Cover the blade of the sword with silver duct tape. Cover the cross guard and pommel with black duct tape.

Step 8: Glue the fake jewels on the hilt of the sword for decoration.

Tip: Research Viking warriors at the library or on the Internet to get ideas for decorating your gear.

Giant Cardboard Fortress

Lords and ladies of the kingdom need a cool place to hang out. **Collect large cardboard boxes and tubes to make your own fortress. Use appliance boxes to make your fortress big enough for some knights and their horses too.**

MATERIALS

- 4 large cardboard refrigerator boxes
- several large flat sheets of cardboard
- large cardboard tubes
- tissue boxes
- duct tape
- heavy string
- light gray paint
- thick black markers

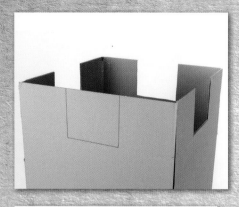

Step 1: Use the refrigerator boxes to make the corner towers of the fortress. Open the tops and use duct tape to hold the side flaps open. Measure and mark a line 5 inches (13 cm) from the top on each side. Measure and mark 6-inch (15-cm) long rectangles along the line. Cut out every other rectangle to make fortress battlements.

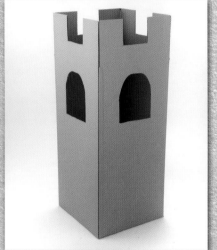

Step 2: Draw arched windows on the outer walls of the towers. Cut them out. Use duct tape to attach the flat sheets of cardboard between the towers to form fortress walls.

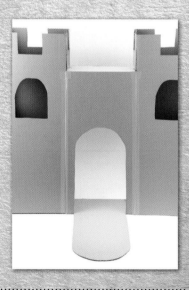

Step 3: Draw and cut out a large arched door on the front of the fortress. Leave the base of the door uncut to make a drawbridge.

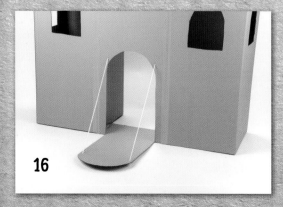

16

Step 4: Punch holes on each side of the doorway and at the top of the drawbridge as shown. Tie strings to the top of the drawbridge and thread them through the holes above the doorway. Tie knots in the ends of the strings to hold them in place.

Step 5: Add flagpoles to the fortress by taping the cardboard tubes to the top of the walls. To make flags, cut out cardboard flag shapes and glue or tape them to the cardboard tubes.

Step 6: Add balconies to some windows by taping tissue boxes beneath them.

Step 7: Paint the entire castle light gray. Paint the flags red or blue.

Step 8: When the paint is dry, draw rectangle shapes with a thick black marker to look like stone blocks. You can also add royal emblems and crests to the flags. Now gather your friends together to help defend the fortress and your kingdom!

17

Homemade Movie Projector

With this cool homemade projector, you can make your own movie theater at home! Set up some comfortable chairs in a dark room, gather some friends, and start the show. Don't forget the popcorn!

MATERIALS

- shoe box with lid
- black paint
- small magnifying glass
- smartphone
- modeling clay

Step 1: Paint the inside of the shoe box and the lid black.

Step 2: In one end of the box, cut a hole slightly smaller than the magnifying glass.

Step 3: Use duct tape or hot glue to attach the magnifying glass over the hole inside the box.

Step 4: Put the box on a table in a dark room and point it toward an empty wall. Open a photo on the smartphone and place the phone near the opposite end of the box. Use modeling clay to hold it in place.

Step 5: Put the lid on the box. The image on the phone will be projected onto the wall. If the image is upside down, flip the phone over inside the box. Adjust the distance between the box and the wall to focus the picture. Now start a movie on the phone, kick back, and enjoy the show!

Super Solar Cooker

Summer sunshine can get pretty hot. Why not use that solar energy to make a fun lunch with your friends? With this solar cooker, you can roast hot dogs and make s'mores without even building a campfire.

MATERIALS

- clean pizza box with lid
- aluminum foil
- clear tape
- plastic wrap
- black construction paper
- newspaper

Step 1: Cover the inside bottom of the pizza box with black construction paper. The black paper helps absorb heat from the sun. Roll up sheets of newspaper and tape them around the edges inside the box. The newspaper helps insulate the cooker.

Step 2: Close the pizza box. Then measure and mark a 1-inch (2.5-cm) wide border on the front, left, and right sides of the box top. Ask an adult to help cut along the marks to make a flap. Fold the flap up.

Step 3: Cover the inside of the flap with aluminum foil. Be sure the shiny side faces out to reflect the sun.

Step 4: Tape two sheets of plastic wrap over the hole in the lid. Make sure the plastic wrap is sealed completely.

Step 5: At about noon or when the sun is hottest, open the box and place your food inside at the center. Then close the lid tightly and prop up the flap. Place the box so the flap reflects sunlight onto the food. When your food looks ready, remove and enjoy!

Magic Money Mover

How does the dollar bill move from one side of the wallet to the other? With just a few simple supplies, you can create this fun magical wallet to astound your family and friends.

MATERIALS

- 1 sheet of cardboard
- 2 pieces of blue ribbon, 4 inches (10 cm) long
- 2 pieces of white ribbon, 4 inches (10 cm) long
- clear tape
- ruler
- dollar bill

Step 1: Cut two rectangles of cardboard measuring 2.75 by 4 inches (7 by 10 cm). Lay the blue ribbons across the top and bottom of one rectangle. The ribbons should be about 0.25 inch (0.6 cm) from the top and bottom edges. The ribbon ends will extend about 0.5 inch (1.3 cm) past each side.

Step 2: Place the second cardboard rectangle on top of the first so the ribbons are between them. Fold the ends of the ribbons on the right side over the top and tape in place.

Step 3: Flip the cardboard sandwich over. Fold the ends of the ribbon over the top piece and tape in place.

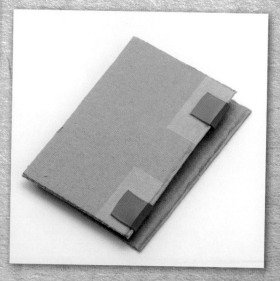

Step 4: Unfold the cardboard pieces. The ribbon will run between the rectangles. The piece on the right has ribbons taped to the underside. The piece on the left has ribbons taped to the top.

Step 5: Place the white ribbons in an X shape on the right rectangle. Tuck the ends of the white ribbon under the left rectangle.

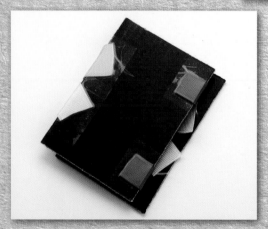

Step 6: Flip the left rectangle over the right rectangle. Fold the ends of the white ribbon on the left side over the top and tape them down.

Step 7: Flip the whole wallet over. Fold the ends of the white ribbon on the right side over the top rectangle and tape them down.

24

Step 8: Open the wallet. There will be two lines of blue ribbon on the left, and an X of white ribbon on the right.

Step 9: Place a folded dollar bill on top of the X and close the wallet. Open it from left to right. The dollar moves under the X! Close the wallet and open it from left to right again. The dollar bill moves to the other side.

Tip: Cover the backsides of the magic wallet with colored paper to hide the taped ribbon ends.

Colossal Cardboard Ball

Here's a riddle for you. What do you get when you join 30 flat cardboard squares at the corners? A big sphere! This cardboard ball is not only super cool, it's quick and easy to make.

MATERIALS

- 30 squares of sturdy cardboard, 10 by 10 inches (25 by 25 cm)
- 60 brass fasteners

Step 1: Punch a hole in each corner of all the cardboard squares.

Step 2: Use brass fasteners to join five squares at the corners to make a pentagon-shaped space in the center.

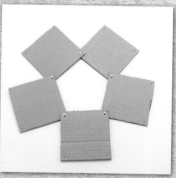

Step 3: On the outer corners of the first squares, add more squares to make triangle-shaped spaces between them.

Step 4: Continue adding squares until you have used all 30. Arrange them so the spaces alternate between pentagons and triangles. Gently curve each row of squares until you have a sphere shape.

Tip: Take your colossal ball outside on a windy day and watch as the air pushes it along. It seems to almost move by itself!

Armored Knight Costume

Thinking of joining in on some cardboard combat? This cardboard armor can help protect you. Suit up and get ready for battle!

MATERIALS

- cardboard box about the size of your upper body
- large paper plate
- pencil
- silver duct tape
- silver paint
- black marker
- string
- buttons or bottle caps

Step 1: Cut off one short side of the cardboard box. Using the plate as a pattern, draw a circle on the other short side large enough for your head. Cut out the circle.

Step 2: Put the cardboard on over your head like a poncho. Have a friend draw lines to mark out the waistline and armholes. Take the box off and cut the cardboard at the markings. The box should now look like an undershirt.

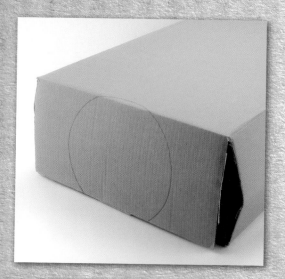

Step 3: Try on the armor shirt and bend the sides to adjust it as needed. Use duct tape to hold the sides together if necessary.

Step 4: Paint the armor silver. Use markers to add a crest or logo to the front.

Step 5: For the helmet, use a piece of string to measure around your head. Cut four 1-inch (2.5-cm) wide strips of cardboard to the measured length. Hot glue the ends of one strip together to make a hoop that fits around your head. There should be a little wiggle room.

Step 6: Bend another cardboard strip into an upside down U shape. Glue the ends to the inside of the circle to form the top of the helmet. Repeat with another cardboard strip. Make it cross the first strip at the center top of the helmet. Trim away the ends that hang down under the edge of the circle.

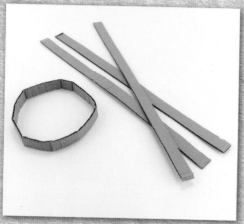

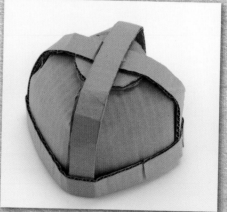

Step 7: Cut a 3-inch (7.6-cm) wide cardboard circle. Glue it under the cross point at the top of the helmet.

Step 8: Cut four triangles with rounded corners to fit inside the open spaces in the frame. Hot glue them to the inside of the frame.

Step 9: Cut a U-shaped piece of cardboard to use as a face shield. Cut smaller U shapes for eyeholes.

Step 10: Hot glue the face shield inside the front of the helmet rim. Glue a strip of 1-inch (2.5-cm) wide cardboard between the eyeholes to form a nose guard.

Step 11: Hot glue metal buttons or bottle caps to look like rivets in the helmet frame. Paint the helmet silver and let it dry. Now put on your armor and helmet, grab your sword and shield, and get ready for battle!

Tip: To make the armor more flexible, try cutting open the box sides. Then punch holes in the sides and lace them together with heavy string.

Read More

Enz, Tammy. *Build Your Own Periscope, Flashlight, and Other Useful Stuff*. Build It Yourself. Mankato, Minn.: Capstone Press, 2011.

Jones, Jen. *Cool Crafts with Cardboard and Wrapping Paper: Green Projects for Resourceful Kids*. Green Crafts. Mankato, Minn.: Capstone Press, 2011.

Kings, Gary. *Funky Junk: Recycle Rubbish into Art!* Mineola, N.Y.: Dover Publications, 2012.

MacNeal, Noel. *Box!: Castles, Kitchens, and Other Cardboard Creations for Kids*. Guilford, Conn.: Lyons Press, 2013.

Internet Sites

FactHound offers a safe, fun way to find Internet sites related to this book. All of the sites on FactHound have been researched by our staff.

Here's all you do:

Visit *www.facthound.com*

Type in this code: 9781491442913

 **Super-cool stuff!** Check out projects, games and lots more at **www.capstonekids.com**